Tertullian

On Baptism

Tertullian

On Baptism

Tertullian
On Baptism

Published by
Lighthouse Christian Publishing
SAN 257-4330
5531 Dufferin Drive
Savage, Minnesota, 55378
United States of America

www.lighthousechristianpublishing.com

Tertullian

Introductory Note.

The Second Class of Tertullian's works, according to the logical method I have endeavored to carry out, is that which includes his treatises against the heresies of his times. In these, the genius of our author is brilliantly illustrated, while, in melancholy fact, he is demonstrating the folly of his own final lapse and the wickedness of that schism and heresy into which he fell away from Truth. Were it not that history abounds in like examples of the frailty of the human intellect and of the insufficiency of "man that walketh to direct his steps," we should be forced to a theory of mental decay to account for inconsistencies so gross and for delusions so besotted. "Genius to madness is *indeed* allied," and who knows but something like that imbecility which closed the career of Swift may have been the fate of this splendid wit and versatile man of parts? Charity, admiration and love force this inquiry upon my own mind continually, as I explore his fascinating pages. And the order in which the student will find them in this series, will lead, I think, to similar reflections on the part of many readers. We observe a natural bent and turn of mind, even in his Catholic writings, which indicate his perils. These are more and more apparent in his recent works, as his enthusiasm heats itself into a frenzy which at last becomes a rage. He breaks down by degrees, as in orthodoxy so also in force and in character. It is almost like the collapse of Solomon or of Bacon. And though our own times have produced no example of stars of equal magnitude, to become falling-stars, we have seen illustrations the most humiliating, of those calm words of Bishop Kaye: "Human nature often presents the curious phenomenon of a union of the most opposite qualities in the same mind; of vigor, acuteness and discrimination on some subjects, with imbecility, dullness and bigotry on others." Milton, himself another example of his own threnode, breaks forth in this splendid utterance of lyrical confession:

"God of our fathers what is man?
Nor do I name of men the common rout,
That, wandering loose about,
Grow up and perish as the summer fly,
Heads without name, no more remembered,
But such as thou hast solemnly elected,
With gifts and graces eminently adorned,
To some great work, thy glory
And people's safety, *which in part they effect*."

And here, I must venture a remark on the ambiguity of the expressions concerning our author's Montanism. In the treatise against Marcion, written late in his career, Tertullian identifies himself with the Church and strenuously defends its faith and its apostolic order. In only rare instances does his weakness for the "new prophecy" crop out, and then, it is only as one identifies himself with a school within the church. Precisely so Fenelon maintained his milder Montanism, without a thought of deserting the Latin Church. Afterwards Fenelon drew back, but at last poor Tertullian fell away. So with the Jansenists. They credited the *miracles* and the *convulsions* (or ecstasies) of their school, and condemned those who rejected them, as Tertullian condemns the *Psychics*. The great expounder of the Nicene Faith (Bp. Bull) does indeed speak very decidedly of Tertullian as a *lapser*, even when he wrote his first book against Marcion. His semi-schismatic position must be allowed. But, was it a *formal* lapse at that time? The English non-jurors were long in communion with the Church, even while they denounced their brethren and the "Erastianizing" clergy, much as Tertullian does the *Psychics*. St. Augustine speaks of *Tertullianists* with great moderation, and notes the final downfall of our author as something distinct from Tertullianism. When we reflect, therefore, that only four of all his varied writings (now extant) are proofs of an accomplished lapse, ought we not carefully to maintain the distinction between the Montanistic Tertullian and Tertullian the Montanist? Bishop Bull, it seems to me would not object to this way of putting it, when we consider his own discrimination in the following weighty words. He says:

"A clear distinction must be made between those works which Tertullian, when already a Montanist, wrote specifically in defense of Montanism *against the church*, and those which he composed, as a Montanist indeed, yet *not in defense of Montanism against the church*, but rather, *in defense of the common doctrines of the church*—and of Montanus, in opposition to other heretics."

Now in arranging the works of this second class, *the Prescription* comes logically first, because, written in Orthodoxy, it forcibly upholds the Scriptural Rule of Faith, the Catholic touchstone of all professed verity. It is also a necessary Introduction to the great work against Marcion which I have placed next in order; giving it the precedence to which it is entitled in part on chronological ground, in part because of the general purity of its material with the exhibition it presents of the author's mental processes and of his very gradual decline from Truth.

Very fortunate were the Edinburgh Editors in securing for this work and some others, the valuable labors of Dr. Holmes, of whom I have elsewhere given some biographical

particulars. The merit and fullness of his annotations are so marked, that I have been spared a great deal of work, such as I was forced to bestow on the former volumes of this American Edition. But on the other hand these pages have given me much patient study and toil as an editor, because of the "shreds and patches" in which Tertullian comes to us, in the Edinburgh Series; and because of some typographical peculiarities, exceptional in that Series itself, and presenting complications, when transferred to a new form of mechanical arrangement.
For example, apart from some valuable material which belongs to the General Preface, and which I have transferred accordingly, the following dislocations confronted me to begin with: The *Marcion* is presented to us in Volume VII. apart from the other writings of Tertullian. At the close of Vol. XI. we reach the *Ad Nationes*, of which Dr. Holmes is the translator, another hand (Mr. Thelwall's) having been employed on former pages of that volume. It is not till we reach Volume XV. that Tertullian again appears, but this volume is wholly the work of Dr. Holmes. Finally, in Volume XVIII., we meet Tertullian again, (Mr. Thelwall the able translator), but, here is placed the "Introduction" to all the works of
Tertullian, which, of course, I have, transferred to its proper place. I make these explanations by no means censoriously, but to point out at once the nature of my own task, and the advantage that accrues to the reader, by the order in which the works of the great Tertullian appear in this edition, enabling him to compare different or parallel passages, all methodically arranged in consecutive pages, without a minute's search, or delay.

Now, as to typographical difficulties to which I have referred, Dr. Holmes marks all his multiplied and useful notes with *brackets*, which are almost always superfluous, and which in this American Edition are used to designate my own contributions, when printed with the text, or apart from Preface and Elucidations. These, therefore, I have removed necessarily and with no appreciable loss to the work, but great gain to the

beauty of the page. But, again, Dr. Holmes' translations are all so heavily bracketed as to become an eyesore, and the disfigured pages have been often complained of as afflictive to the reader. Many words strictly implied by the original Latin, and which should therefore be unmarked, are yet put between brackets. Even minute words (*and*, or *to wit*, or *again*,) when, in the nature of the case the English idiom requires them, are thus marked. I have not retained these blemishes; but when an inconsiderable word or a repetition does add to the sense, or qualify it, I have italicized such words, throwing more important interpolations into parenthetical marks, which are less painful to the sight than brackets. I have found them quite as serviceable to denote the auxiliary word or phrase; and where the author himself uses a parenthesis, I have observed very few instances in which a sensible reader would confound it with the translator's efforts to eke out the sense. Sometimes, an awkward interpolation has been thrown into a footnote.
Occasionally the crabbed sentences of the great Carthaginian are so obscure that Dr. Holmes has been unable to make them lucid, although, with the original in hand, he probably felt a force in his own rendering which the mere English reader must fail to perceive. In a few such instances, noting the fact in the margin, I have tried to bring out the sense, by slight modifications of punctuation and arrangement. Occasionally too I have dropped a superfluous interpolation (such as *e.g.*, *to conclude*, or let me say again,) when I have found that it only served to clog and overcharge a sentence. Last of all, Dr. Holmes' *headings* have sometimes been condensed, to avoid phrases and sentences immediately recurring in the chapter. These purely mechanical parts require a terse form of statement, like those in the English Bible, and I have frequently reduced them on that model, dropping redundant adverbs and adjectives to bring out the catchwords.

On Baptism.

Chapter I.— Introduction. Origin of the Treatise.

Happy is our sacrament of water, in that, by washing away the sins of our early blindness, we are set free and admitted into eternal life! A treatise on this matter will not be superfluous; instructing not only such as are just becoming formed (in the faith), but them who, content with having simply believed, without full examination of the grounds of the traditions, carry (in mind), through ignorance, an untried though probable faith. The consequence is, that a viper of the Cainite heresy, lately conversant in this quarter, has carried away a great number with her most venomous doctrine, making it her first aim to destroy baptism. Which is quite in accordance with nature; for vipers and asps and basilisks themselves generally do affect arid and waterless places. But we, little fishes, after the example of our ΙΧΘΥΣ Jesus Christ, are born in water, nor have we safety in any other way than by permanently abiding in water; so that most monstrous creature, who had no right to teach even sound doctrine, knew full well how to kill the little fishes, by taking them away from the water!

Chapter II—The Very Simplicity of God's Means of Working, a Stumbling-Block to the Carnal Mind.

Well, but how great is the force of perversity for so shaking the faith or entirely preventing its reception, that it impugns it on the very principles of which the faith consists! There is absolutely nothing which makes men's minds more obdurate than the simplicity of the divine works which are visible in the act, when compared with the grandeur which is promised thereto in the effect; so that from the very fact, that with so great simplicity, without pomp, without any considerable novelty of preparation, finally, without expense, a man is dipped in water, and amid the utterance of some few words, is sprinkled, and then rises again, not much (or not at all) the cleaner, the consequent attainment of eternity is esteemed the more incredible. I am a deceiver if, on the contrary, it is not from their circumstance, and preparation, and expense, that idols' solemnities or mysteries get their credit and authority built up. Oh, miserable incredulity, which quite denies to God His own properties, simplicity and power! What then? Is it not wonderful, too, that death should be washed away by bathing? But it is the more to be believed if the wonderfulness be the reason why it is not believed. For what does it behoove divine works to be in their quality, except that they be above all wonder? We also ourselves wonder, but it is because we believe. Incredulity, on the other hand, wonders, but does not believe: for the simple acts it wonders at, as if they were vain; the grand results, as if they were impossible. And grant that it be just as you think sufficient to meet each point is the divine declaration which has forerun: "The foolish things of the world hath God elected to confound its wisdom;" and, "The things very difficult with men are easy with God." For if God is wise and powerful (which even they who pass Him by do not deny), it is with good reason that He lays the material causes of His own operation in the contraries of wisdom and of power, that is, in foolishness and impossibility; since every virtue receives its cause from those things by which it is called forth.

Chapter III—Water Chosen as a Vehicle of Divine Operation and Wherefore. Its Prominence First of All in Creation.

Mindful of this declaration as of a conclusive prescript, we nevertheless proceed to treat the question, "How foolish and impossible it is to be formed anew by water. In what respect, pray, has this material substance merited an office of so high dignity?" The authority, I suppose, of the liquid element has to be examined. This however, is found in abundance, and that from the very beginning. For water is one of those things which, before all the furnishing of the world, were quiescent with God in a yet unshapen state. "In the first beginning," saith Scripture, "God made the heaven and the earth. But the earth was invisible, and unorganized, and darkness was over the abyss; and the Spirit of the Lord was hovering over the waters." The first thing, O man, which you have to venerate, is the age of the waters in that their substance is ancient; the second, their dignity, in that they were the seat of the Divine Spirit, more pleasing to Him, no doubt, than all the other then existing elements. For the darkness was total thus far, shapeless, without the ornament of stars; and the abyss gloomy; and the earth unfurnished; and the heaven unwrought: water alone—always a perfect, gladsome, simple material substance, pure in itself—supplied a worthy vehicle to God. What of the fact that waters were in some way the regulating powers by which the disposition of the world thenceforward was constituted by God? For the suspension of the celestial firmament in the midst He caused by "dividing the waters;" the suspension of "the dry land" He accomplished by "separating the waters." After the world had been hereupon set in order through its elements, when inhabitants were given it, "the waters" were the first to receive the precept "to bring forth living creatures." Water was the first to produce that which had life, that it might be no wonder in baptism if waters know how to give life. For was not the work of fashioning man himself also achieved with the aid of waters? Suitable material is found in the earth, yet not apt for the purpose unless it be moist and juicy; which (earth) "the waters," separated the fourth day before into their own place, temper with their remaining moisture to a clayey consistency. If, from that time onward, I go forward in recounting universally, or at more length, the evidences of the "authority" of this element which I can adduce to show how great is its power or its grace; how many ingenious devices, how many functions, how useful an instrumentality, it affords the world, I fear I may seem to have collected rather the praises of water than the reasons of baptism; although I should thereby teach all the more fully, that it is not to be doubted that God has made the material substance which He has disposed throughout all His products and works, obey Him also in His own peculiar sacraments; that the material substance which governs terrestrial life acts as agent likewise in the celestial.

Chapter IV—The Primeval Hovering of the Spirit of God Over the Waters Typical of Baptism. The Universal Element of Water Thus Made a Channel of Sanctification. Resemblance Between the Outward Sign and the Inward Grace.

But it will suffice to have thus called at the outset those points in which withal is recognized that primary principle of baptism—which was even then fore-noted by the very attitude assumed for a type of baptism, —that the Spirit of God, who hovered over (the waters) from the beginning, would continue to linger over the waters of the baptized. But a holy thing, of course, hovered over a holy; or else, from that which hovered over that which was hovered over borrowed a holiness, since it is necessary that in every case an underlying material substance should catch the quality of that which overhangs it, most of all a corporeal of a spiritual, adapted (as the spiritual is) through the subtleness of its substance, both for penetrating and insinuating. Thus the nature of the waters, sanctified by the Holy One, itself conceived withal the power of sanctifying. Let no one say, "Why then, are we, pray, baptized with the very waters which then existed in the first beginning?" Not with those waters, of course, except in so far as the genus indeed is one, but the species very many. But what is an attribute to the genus reappears likewise in the species. And accordingly it makes no difference whether a man be washed in a sea or a pool, a stream or a fount, a lake or a trough; nor is there any distinction between those whom John baptized in the Jordan and those whom Peter baptized in the Tiber, unless withal the eunuch whom Philip baptized in the midst of his journeys with chance water, derived (therefrom) more or less of salvation than others. All waters, therefore, in virtue of the pristine privilege of their origin, do, after invocation of God, attain the sacramental power of sanctification; for the Spirit immediately supervenes from the heavens, and rests over the waters, sanctifying them from Himself; and being thus sanctified, they imbibe at the same time the power of sanctifying. Albeit the similitude may be admitted to be suitable to the simple act; that, since we are defiled by sins, as it were by dirt, we should be washed from those stains in waters. But as sins do not show themselves in our flesh (inasmuch as no one carries on his skin the spot of idolatry, or fornication, or fraud), so persons of that kind are foul in the spirit, which is the author of the sin; for the spirit is lord, the flesh servant. Yet they each mutually share the guilt: the spirit, on the ground of command; the flesh, of subservience. Therefore, after the waters have been in a manner endued with medicinal virtue through the intervention of the angel, the spirit is corporeally washed in the waters, and the flesh is in the same spiritually cleansed.

Chapter V.—Use Made of Water by the Heathen. Type of the Angel at the Pool of Bethsaida.

"Well, but the nations, who are strangers to all understanding of spiritual powers, ascribe to their idols the imbuing of waters with the self-same efficacy." (So they do) but they cheat themselves with waters which are widowed. For washing is the channel through which they are initiated into some sacred rites—of some notorious Isis or Mithras. The gods themselves likewise they honor by washings. Moreover, by carrying water around, and sprinkling it, they everywhere expiate country-seats, houses, temples, and whole cities: at all events, at the Apollinarian and Eleusinian games they are baptized; and they presume that the effect of their doing that is their regeneration and the remission of the penalties due to their perjuries. Among the ancients, again, whoever had defiled himself with murder, was wont to go in quest of purifying waters. Therefore, if the mere nature of water, in that it is the appropriate material for washing away, leads men to flatter themselves with a belief in omens of purification, how much more truly will waters render that service through the authority of God, by whom all their nature has been constituted! If men think that water is endued with a medicinal virtue by religion, what religion is more effectual than that of the living God? Which fact being acknowledged, we recognize here also the zeal of the devil rivalling the things of God, while we find him, too, practicing baptism in his subjects. What similarity is there? The unclean cleanses! the ruiner sets free! the damned absolves! He will, forsooth, destroy his own work, by washing away the sins which himself inspires! These (remarks) have been set down by way of testimony against such as reject the faith; if they put no trust in the things of God, the spurious imitations of which, in the case of God's rival, they do trust in. Are there not other cases too, in which, without any sacrament, unclean spirits brood on waters, in spurious imitation of that brooding of the Divine Spirit in the very beginning? Witness all shady founts, and all unfrequented brooks, and the ponds in the baths, and the conduits in private houses, or the cisterns and wells which are said to have the property of "spiriting away," through the power, that is, of a hurtful spirit. Men whom waters have drowned or affected with madness or with fear, they call nymph caught, or "lymphatic," or "hydro-phobic." Why have we adduced these instances? Lest any think it too hard for belief that a holy angel of God should grant his presence to waters, to temper them to man's salvation; while the evil angel holds frequent profane commerce with the selfsame element to man's ruin. If it seems a novelty for an angel to be present in waters, an example of what was to come to pass has forerun. An angel, by his intervention, was wont to stir the pool at Bethsaida. They who were complaining of ill-health used to watch for him; for whoever had been the first to descend into them, after his washing, ceased to complain. This figure of corporeal healing sang of a spiritual healing, according to the rule by which things carnal are always antecedent as figurative of things spiritual. And thus, when the grace of God advanced to higher degrees among men, an accession of efficacy was granted to the waters and to the angel. They who were wont to remedy bodily defects, now heal the spirit; they who used to work temporal salvation now renew eternal; they who did set free but once in the year, now save peoples in a body daily, death being done away through ablution of sins. The guilt being removed, of course the penalty is removed too. Thus man will be restored for God to His "likeness," who in days bygone had been conformed to "the image" of God; (the "image" is counted (to be) in his form: the "likeness" in his eternity:) for he receives again that Spirit of God which he had then first received from His afflatus, but had afterward lost through sin.

Chapter VI—The Angel the Forerunner of the Holy Spirit. Meaning Contained in the Baptismal Formula.

Not that in the waters we obtain the Holy Spirit; but in the water, under (the witness of) the angel, we are cleansed, and prepared for the Holy Spirit. In this case also a type has preceded; for thus was John beforehand the Lord's forerunner, "preparing His ways." Thus, too, does the angel, the witness of baptism, "make the paths straight" for the Holy Spirit, who is about to come upon us, by the washing away of sins, which faith, sealed in (the name of) the Father, and the Son, and the Holy Spirit, obtains. For if "in the mouth of three witnesses every word shall stand:"—while, through the benediction, we have the same (three) as witnesses of our faith whom we have as sureties of our salvation too—how much more does the number of the divine names suffice for the assurance of our hope likewise! Moreover, after the pledging both of the attestation of faith and the promise of salvation under "three witnesses," there is added, of necessity, mention of the Church;

inasmuch as, wherever there are three, (that is, the Father, the Son, and the Holy Spirit,) there is the Church, which is a body of three.

Chapter VII—Of the Unction.

After this, when we have issued from the font, we are thoroughly anointed with a blessed unction— (a practice derived) from the old discipline, wherein on entering the priesthood, men were wont to be anointed with oil from a horn, ever since Aaron was anointed by Moses. Whence Aaron is called "Christ," from the "chrism," which is "the unction;" which, when made spiritual, furnished an appropriate name to the Lord, because He was "anointed" with the Spirit by God the Father; as written in the Acts: "For truly they were gathered together in this city against Thy Holy Son whom Thou hast anointed." Thus, too, in our case, the unction runs carnally, (i.e. on the body,) but profits spiritually; in the same way as the act of baptism itself too is carnal, in that we are plunged in water, but the effect spiritual, in that we are freed from sins.

Chapter VIII—Of the Imposition of Hands. Types of the Deluge and the Dove.

In the next place the hand is laid on us, invoking and inviting the Holy Spirit through benediction. Shall it be granted possible for human ingenuity to summon a spirit into water, and, by the application of hands from above, to animate their union into one body with another spirit of so clear sound; and shall it not be possible for God, in the case of His own organ, to produce, by means of "holy hands," a sublime spiritual modulation? But this, as well as the former, is derived from the old sacramental rite in which Jacob blessed his grandsons, born of Joseph, Ephrem and Manasses; with his hands laid on them and interchanged, and indeed so transversely slanted one over the other, that, by delineating Christ, they even portended the future benediction into Christ. Then, over our cleansed and blessed bodies willingly descends from the Father that Holiest Spirit. Over the waters of baptism, recognizing as it were His primeval seat, He reposes: (He who) glided down on the Lord "in the shape of a dove," in order that the nature of the Holy Spirit might be declared by means of the creature (the emblem) of simplicity and innocence, because even in her bodily structure the dove is without literal gall. And accordingly He says, "Be ye simple as doves." Even this is not without the supporting evidence of a preceding figure. For just as, after the waters of the deluge, by which the old iniquity was purged—after the baptism, so to say, of the world—a dove was the herald which announced to the earth the assuagement of celestial wrath, when she had been sent her way out of the ark, and had returned with the olive-branch, a sign which even among the nations is the fore-token of peace; so by the self-same law of heavenly effect, to earth—that is, to our flesh—as it emerges from the font, after its old sins flies the dove of the Holy Spirit, bringing us the peace of God, sent out from the heavens where is the Church, the typified ark. But the world returned unto sin; in which point baptism would ill be compared to the deluge. And so it is destined to fire; just as the man too is, who after baptism renews his sins: so that this also ought to be accepted as a sign for our admonition.

Chapter IX—Types of the Red Sea, and the Water from the Rock.

How many, therefore, are the pleas of nature, how many the privileges of grace, how many the solemnities of discipline, the figures, the preparations, the prayers, which have ordained the sanctity of water? First, indeed, when the people, set unconditionally free, escaped the violence of the Egyptian king by crossing over through water, it was water that extinguished the king himself, with his entire forces. What figure more manifestly fulfilled in the sacrament of baptism?

The nations are set free from the world by means of water, to wit: and the devil, their old tyrant, they leave quite behind, overwhelmed in the water. Again, water is restored from its defect of "bitterness" to its native grace of "sweetness" by the tree of Moses. That tree was Christ, restoring, to wit, of Himself, the veins of sometime envenomed and bitter nature into the all-salutary waters of baptism. This is the water which flowed continuously down for the people from the "accompanying rock;" for if Christ is "the Rock," without doubt we see baptism blest by the water in Christ. How mighty is the grace of water, in the sight of God and His Christ, for the confirmation of baptism! Never is Christ without water: if, that is, He is Himself baptized in water; inaugurates in water the first rudimentary displays of His power, when invited to the nuptials; invites the thirsty, when He makes a discourse, to His own sempiternal water; approves, when teaching concerning love, among works of charity, the cup of water offered to a poor (child); recruits His strength at a well; walks over the water; willingly crosses the sea; ministers water to His disciples. Onward even to the passion does the witness of baptism last: while He is being surrendered to the cross, water intervenes; witness Pilate's hands: when He is wounded, forth from His side bursts water; witness the soldier's lance!

Chapter X.—Of John's Baptism.

We have spoken, so far as our moderate ability permitted, of the generals which form the groundwork of the sanctity of baptism. I will now, equally to the best of my power, proceed to the rest of its character, touching certain minor questions.

The baptism announced by John formed the subject, even at that time, of a question, proposed by the Lord Himself indeed to the Pharisees, whether that baptism was heavenly, or truly earthly: about which they were unable to give a consistent answer, inasmuch as they understood not, because they believed not. But we, with but as poor a measure of understanding as of faith, are able to determine that that baptism was divine indeed, (yet in respect of the command, not in respect of efficacy too, in that we read that John was sent by the Lord to perform this duty,) but human in its nature: for it conveyed nothing celestial, but it fore-ministered to things celestial; being, to wit, appointed over repentance, which is in man's power. In fact, the doctors of the law and the Pharisees, who were unwilling to "believe," did not "repent" either. But if repentance is a thing human, its baptism must necessarily be of the same nature: else, if it had been celestial, it would have given both the Holy Spirit and remission of sins. But none either pardons sins or freely grants the Spirit save God only. Even the Lord Himself said that the Spirit would not descend on any other condition, but that He should first ascend to the Father. What the Lord was not yet conferring, of course the servant could not furnish. Accordingly, in the Acts of the Apostles, we find that men who had "John's baptism" had not received the Holy Spirit, whom they knew not even by hearing. That, then, was no celestial thing which furnished no celestial (endowments): whereas the very thing which was celestial in John—the Spirit of prophecy—so completely failed, after the transfer of the whole Spirit to the Lord, that he presently sent to inquire whether He whom he had himself preached, whom he had pointed out when coming to him, were "HE." And so "the baptism of repentance" was dealt with as if it were a candidate for the remission and sanctification shortly about to follow in Christ: for in that John used to preach "baptism for the remission of sins," the declaration was made with reference to future remission; if it be true, (as it is,) that repentance is antecedent, remission subsequent; and this is "preparing the way." But he who "prepares" does not himself "perfect," but procures for another to perfect. John himself professes that the celestial things are not his, but Christ's, by saying, "He who is from the earth speaketh concerning the earth; He who comes from the realms above is above all;" and again, by saying that he "baptized in repentance only, but that One would shortly come who would baptize in the Spirit and fire;"—of course because true and stable faith is baptized with water, unto salvation; pretended and weak faith is baptized with fire, unto judgment.

Chapter XI—Answer to the Objection that "The Lord Did Not Baptize."

"But behold, "say some, "the Lord came, and baptized not; for we read, 'And yet He used not to baptize, but His disciples!'" As if, in truth, John had preached that He would baptize with His own hands! Of course, his words are not so to be understood, but as simply spoken after an ordinary manner; just as, for instance, we say, "The emperor set forth an edict," or, "The prefect cudgeled him." Pray does the emperor in person set forth, or the prefect in person cudgel? One whose ministers do a thing is always said to do it. So "He will baptize you" will have to be understood as standing for, "Through Him," or "Into Him," "you will be baptized." But let not (the fact) that "He Himself baptized not" trouble any. For into whom should He baptize? Into repentance? Of what use, then, do you make His forerunner? Into remission of sins, which He used to give by a word? Into Himself, whom by humility He was concealing? Into the Holy Spirit, who had not yet descended from the Father? Into the Church, which His apostles had not yet founded? And thus it was with the selfsame "baptism of John" that His disciples used to baptize, as ministers, with which John before had baptized as forerunner. Let none think it was with some other, because no other exists, except that of Christ subsequently; which at that time, of course, could not be given by His disciples, inasmuch as the glory of the Lord had not yet been fully attained, nor the efficacy of the font established through the passion and the resurrection; because neither can our death see dissolution except by the Lord's passion, nor our life be restored without His resurrection.

Chapter XII—Of the Necessity of Baptism to Salvation.

When, however, the prescript is laid down that "without baptism, salvation is attainable by none" (chiefly on the ground of that declaration of the Lord, who says, "Unless one be born of water, he hath not life"), there arise immediately scrupulous, nay rather audacious, doubts on the part of some, "how, in accordance with that prescript, salvation is attainable by the apostles, whom—Paul excepted—we do not find baptized in the Lord? Nay, since Paul is the only one of them who has put on the garment of Christ's baptism, either the peril of all the others who lack the water of Christ is prejudged, that the prescript may be maintained, or else the prescript is rescinded if salvation has been ordained even for the unbaptized." I have heard—the Lord is my witness—doubts of that kind: that none may imagine me so abandoned as to excogitate, unprovoked, in the license of my pen, ideas which would inspire others with scruple.

And now, as far as I shall be able, I will reply to them who affirm "that the apostles were unbaptized." For if they had undergone the human baptism of John, and were longing for that of the Lord, then since the Lord Himself had defined baptism to be one; (saying to Peter, who was desirous of being thoroughly bathed, "He who hath once bathed hath no necessity to wash a second time;" which, of course, He would not have said at all to one not baptized;) even here we have a conspicuous proof against those who, in order to destroy the sacrament of water, deprive the apostles even of John's baptism. Can it seem credible that "the way of the Lord," that is, the baptism of John, had not then been "prepared" in those persons who were being destined to open the way of the Lord throughout the whole world? The Lord Himself, though no "repentance" was due from Him, was baptized: was baptism not necessary for sinners? As for the fact, then, that "others were not baptized"—they, however, were not companions of Christ, but enemies of the faith, doctors of the law and Pharisees. From which fact is gathered an additional suggestion, that, since the opposers of the Lord refused to be baptized, they who followed the Lord were baptized, and were not like-minded with their own rivals: especially when, if there were any one to whom they clave, the Lord had exalted John above him (by the testimony) saying, "Among them who are born of women there is none greater than John the Baptist."

Others make the suggestion (forced enough, clearly "that the apostles then served the turn of baptism when in their little ship, were sprinkled and covered with the waves: that Peter himself also was immersed enough when he walked on the sea." It is, however, as I think, one thing to be sprinkled or intercepted by the violence of the sea; another thing to be baptized in obedience to the discipline of religion. But that little ship did present a figure of the Church, in that she is disquieted "in the sea," that is, in the world, "by the waves," that is, by persecutions and temptations; the Lord, through patience, sleeping as it were, until, roused in their last extremities by the prayers of the saints, He checks the world, and restores tranquility to His own.

Now, whether they were baptized in any manner whatever, or whether they continued unbathed to the end—so that even that saying of the Lord touching the "one bath" does, under the person of Peter, merely regard us—still, to determine concerning the salvation of the apostles is audacious enough, because on them the prerogative even of first choice, and thereafter of undivided intimacy, might be able to confer the compendious grace of baptism, seeing they (I think) followed Him who was wont to promise salvation to every believer. "Thy faith," He would say, "hath saved thee;" and, "Thy sins shall be remitted thee," on thy believing, of course, albeit thou be not yet baptized. If that was wanting to the apostles, I know not in the faith of what things it was, that, roused by one word of the Lord, one left the toll-booth behind forever; another deserted father and ship, and the craft by which he gained his living; a third, who disdained his father's obsequies, fulfilled, before he heard it, that highest precept of the Lord, "He who prefers father or mother to me, is not worthy of me."

Chapter XIII—Another Objection: Abraham Pleased God Without Being Baptized. Answer Thereto. Old Things Must Give Place to New, and Baptism is Now a Law.

Here, then, those miscreants provoke questions. And so they say, "Baptism is not necessary for them to whom faith is sufficient; for withal, Abraham pleased God by a sacrament of no water, but of faith." But in all cases it is the later things which have a conclusive force, and the subsequent which prevail over the antecedent. Grant that, in days gone by, there was salvation by means of bare faith, before the passion and resurrection of the Lord. But now that faith has been enlarged, and is become a faith which believes in His nativity, passion, and resurrection, there has been an amplification added to the sacrament, viz., the sealing act of baptism; the clothing, in some sense, of the faith which before was bare, and which cannot exist now without its proper law. For the law of baptizing has been imposed, and the formula prescribed: "Go," He saith, "teach the nations, baptizing them into the name of the Father, and of the Son, and of the Holy Spirit." The comparison with this law of that definition, "Unless a man has been reborn of water and Spirit, he shall not enter into the kingdom of the heavens," has tied faith to the necessity of baptism. Accordingly, all thereafter who became believers used to be baptized. Then it was, too, that Paul, when he believed, was baptized; and this is the meaning of the precept which the Lord had given him when smitten with the plague of loss of sight, saying, "Arise, and enter Damascus; there shall be demonstrated to thee what thou oughtest to do," to wit—be baptized, which was the only thing lacking to him. That point excepted, he had sufficiently learnt and believed "the Nazarene" to be "the Lord, the Son of God."

Chapter XIV—Of Paul's Assertion, that He Had Not Been Sent to Baptize.

But they roll back an objection from that apostle himself, in that he said, "For Christ sent me not to baptize;" as if by this argument baptism were done away! For if so, why did he baptize Gaius, and Crispus, and the house of Stephanas? However, even if Christ had not sent him to baptize, yet He had given other apostles the precept to baptize. But these words were written to the Corinthians in regard of the circumstances of that particular time; seeing that schisms and dissensions were agitated among them, while one attributes everything to Paul, another to Apollos. For which reason the "peace-making" apostle, for fear he should seem to claim all gifts for himself, says that he had been sent "not to baptize, but to preach." For preaching is the prior thing, baptizing the posterior. Therefore, the preaching came first: but I think baptizing withal was lawful to him to whom preaching was.

Chapter XV—Unity of Baptism. Remarks on Heretical and Jewish Baptism.

I know not whether any further point is mooted to bring baptism into controversy. Permit me to call to mind what I have omitted above, lest I seem to break off the train of impending thoughts in the middle. There is to us one, and but one, baptism; as well according to the Lord's gospel as according to the apostle's letters, inasmuch as he says, "One God, and one baptism, and one church in the heavens." But it must be admitted that the question, "What rules are to be observed with regard to heretics?" is worthy of being treated. For it is to us that that assertion refers. Heretics, however, have no fellowship in our discipline, whom the mere fact of their excommunication testifies to be outsiders. I am not bound to recognize in them a thing which is enjoined on me, because they and we have not the same God, nor one—that is, the same—Christ. And therefore their baptism is not one with ours either, because it is not the same; a baptism which, since they have it not duly, doubtless they have not at all; nor is that capable of being counted which is not had. Thus they cannot receive it either, because they have it not. But this point has already received a fuller discussion from us in Greek. We enter, then, the font once: once are sins washed away, because they ought never to be repeated. But the Jewish Israel bathes daily, because he is daily being defiled: and, for fear that defilement should be practiced among us also, therefore was the definition touching the one bathing made. Happy water, which once washes away; which does not mock sinners (with vain hopes); which does not, by being infected with the repetition of impurities, again defile them whom it has washed!

Chapter XVI—Of the Second Baptism—With Blood.

We have indeed, likewise, a second font, (itself withal one with the former,) of blood, to wit; concerning which the Lord said, "I have to be baptized with a baptism," when He had been baptized already. For He had come "by means of water and blood," just as John has written; that He might be baptized by the water, glorified by the blood; to make us, in like manner, called by water, chosen by blood. These two baptisms He sent out from the wound in His pierced side, in order that they who believed in His blood might be bathed with the water; they who had been bathed in the water might likewise drink the blood. This is the baptism which both stands in lieu of the fontal bathing when that has not been received, and restores it when lost.

Chapter XVII—Of the Power of Conferring Baptism.

For concluding our brief subject, it remains to put you in mind also of the due observance of giving and receiving baptism. Of giving it, the chief priest (who is the bishop) has the right: in the next place, the presbyters and deacons, yet not without the bishop's authority, on account of the honor of the Church, which being preserved, peace is preserved. Beside these, even laymen have the right; for what is equally received can be equally given. Unless bishops, or priests, or deacons, be on the spot, other disciples are called i.e. to the work. The word of the Lord ought not to be hidden by any: in like manner, too, baptism, which is equally God's property, can be administered by all. But how much more is the rule of reverence and modesty incumbent on laymen—seeing that these powers belong to their superiors—lest they assume to themselves the specific function of the bishop! Emulation of the episcopal office is the mother of schisms. The most holy apostle has said, that "all things are lawful, but not all expedient." Let it suffice assuredly, in cases of necessity, to avail yourself (of that rule, if at any time circumstance either of place, or of time, or of person compels you (so to do); for then the steadfast courage of the succorer, when the situation of the endangered one is urgent, is exceptionally admissible; inasmuch as he will be guilty of a human creature's loss if he shall refrain from bestowing what he had free liberty to bestow. But the woman of pertness, who has usurped the power to teach, will of course not give birth for herself likewise to a right of baptizing, unless some new beast shall arise like the former; so that, just as the one abolished baptism, so some other should in her own right confer it! But if the writings which wrongly go under Paul's name, claim Thecla's example as a license for women's teaching and baptizing, let them know that, in Asia, the presbyter who composed that writing, as if he were augmenting Paul's fame from his own store, after being convicted, and confessing that he had done it from love of Paul, was removed from his office. For how credible would it seem, that he who has not permitted a woman even to learn with over-boldness, should give a female the power of teaching and of baptizing! "Let them be silent," he says, "and at home consult their own husbands."

Chapter XVIII—Of the Persons to Whom, and the Time When, Baptism is to Be Administered.

But they whose office it is, know that baptism is not rashly to be administered. "Give to everyone who beggeth thee," has a reference of its own, appertaining especially to almsgiving. On the contrary, this precept is rather to be looked at carefully: "Give not the holy thing to the dogs, nor cast your pearls before swine;" and, "Lay not hands easily on any; share not other men's sins." If Philip so "easily" baptized the chamberlain, let us reflect that a manifest and conspicuous evidence that the Lord deemed him worthy had been interposed. The Spirit had enjoined Philip to proceed to that road: the eunuch himself, too, was not found idle, nor as one who was suddenly seized with an eager desire to be baptized; but, after going up to the temple for prayer's sake, being intently engaged on the divine Scripture, was thus suitably discovered—to whom God had, unasked, sent an apostle, which one, again, the Spirit bade adjoin himself to the chamberlain's chariot. The Scripture which he was reading falls in opportunely with his faith: Philip, being requested, is taken to sit beside him; the Lord is pointed out; faith lingers not; water needs no waiting for; the work is completed, and the apostle snatched away. "But Paul too was, in fact, 'speedily' baptized:" for Simon, his host, speedily recognized him to be "an appointed vessel of election." God's approbation sends sure premonitory tokens before it; every "petition" may both deceive and be deceived. And so, according to the circumstances and disposition, and even age, of each individual, the delay of baptism is preferable; principally, however, in the case of little children. For why is it necessary—if (baptism itself) is not so necessary—that the sponsors likewise should be thrust into danger? Who both themselves, by reason of mortality, may fail to fulfil their promises, and may be disappointed by the development of an evil disposition, in those for whom they stood? The Lord does indeed say, "Forbid them not to come unto me." Let them "come," then, while they are growing up; let them "come" while they are learning, while they are learning whither to come; let them become Christians when they have become able to know Christ. Why does the innocent period of life hasten to the "remission of sins?" More caution will be exercised in worldly matters: so that one who is not trusted with earthly substance is trusted with divine! Let them know how to "ask" for salvation, that you may seem (at least) to have given "to him that asketh." For no less cause must the unwedded also be deferred—in whom the ground of temptation is prepared, alike in such as never were wedded by means of their maturity, and in the widowed by means of their freedom—until they either marry, or else be more fully strengthened for continence. If any understand the weighty import of baptism, they will fear its reception more than its delay: sound faith is secure of salvation.

Chapter XIX—Of the Times Most Suitable for Baptism.

The Passover affords a more than usually solemn day for baptism; when, withal, the Lord's passion, in which we are baptized, was completed. Nor will it be incongruous to interpret figuratively the fact that, when the Lord was about to celebrate the last Passover, He said to the disciples who were sent to make preparation, "Ye will meet a man bearing water." He points out the place for celebrating the Passover by the sign of water. After that, Pentecost is a most joyous space for conferring baptisms; wherein, too, the resurrection of the Lord was repeatedly proved among the disciples, and the hope of the advent of the Lord indirectly pointed to, in that, at that time, when He had been received back into the heavens, the angels told the apostles that "He would so come, as He had withal ascended into the heavens;" at Pentecost, of course. But, moreover, when Jeremiah says, "And I will gather them together from the extremities of the land in the feast-day," he signifies the day of the Passover and of Pentecost, which is properly a "feast-day." However, every day is the Lord's; every hour, every time, is apt for baptism: if there is a difference in the solemnity, distinction there is none in the grace.

Chapter XX—Of Preparation for, and Conduct After, the Reception of Baptism.

They who are about to enter baptism ought to pray with repeated prayers, fasts, and bendings of the knee, and vigils all the night through, and with the confession of all bygone sins, that they may express the meaning even of the baptism of John: "They were baptized," saith (the Scripture), "confessing their own sins." To us it is matter for thankfulness if we do now publicly confess our iniquities or our turpitudes: for we do at the same time both make satisfaction for our former sins, by mortification of our flesh and spirit, and lay beforehand the foundation of defenses against the temptations which will closely follow. "Watch and pray," saith (the Lord), "lest ye fall into temptation." And the reason, I believe, why they were tempted was, that they fell asleep; so that they deserted the Lord when apprehended, and he who continued to stand by Him, and used the sword, even denied Him thrice: for withal the word had gone before, that "no one untempted should attain the celestial kingdoms." The Lord Himself forthwith after baptism temptations surrounded, when in forty days He had kept fast. "Then," someone will say, "it becomes us, too, rather to fast after baptism." Well, and who forbids you, unless it be the necessity for joy, and the thanksgiving for salvation? But so far as I, with my poor powers, understand, the Lord figuratively retorted upon Israel the reproach they had cast on the Lord. For the people, after crossing the sea, and being carried about in the desert during forty years, although they were there nourished with divine supplies, nevertheless were more mindful of their belly and their gullet than of God. Thereupon the Lord, driven apart into desert places after baptism, showed, by maintaining a fast of forty days, that the man of God lives "not by bread alone," but "by the word of God;" and that temptations incident to fullness or immoderation of appetite are shattered by abstinence. Therefore, blessed ones, whom the grace of God awaits, when you ascend from that most sacred font of your new birth, and spread your hands for the first time in the house of your mother, together with your brethren, ask from the Father, ask from the Lord, that His own specialties of grace and distributions of gifts may be supplied you. "Ask," saith He, "and ye shall receive." Well, you have asked, and have received; you have knocked, and it has been opened to you. Only, I pray that, when you are asking, you be mindful likewise of Tertullian the sinner.

Elucidation.

The argument (p. 673, note 6,) is conclusive, but not clear. The disciples of John must have been baptized by him, (Luke vii. 29–30) and "all the people," must have included those whom Jesus called. But, this was not Christ's baptism: See Acts xix. 2, 5. Compare note 8, p. 673. And see the American Editor's "Apollos."

www.ingramcontent.com/pod-product-compliance
Lightning Source LLC
Chambersburg PA
CBHW071015120726
47910CB00004B/1529

* 9 7 8 1 6 4 3 7 3 0 8 2 0 *